TEAS, SOUPS & SALADS

HEALING RECIPES FOR SUPPORTIVE MEDICINE

Norman W. Wilson PhD

TEAS, SOUPS & SALADS

HEALING RECIPES FOR
SUPPORTIVE MEDICINE

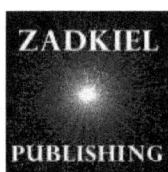

ZADKIEL

PUBLISHING

Cover Design by

www.srwalkerdesigns.com

Zadkiel Publishing
An Imprint of Fiction4All
www.fiction4all.com

This Edition
Published 2020

ALSO BY NORMAN W. WILSON, PhD

Nonfiction:

Shamanism: What it's All About

DUH! The American Educational Disaster

So You THINK You want to be a Buddhist?

Promethean Necessity and Its Implications for Humanity

The Sayings of Esaugetuh, the Master of Breath

Activating Your Spirit Guides

Shamanic Manifesting

The Shaman's Journey through Poetry with Gavriel Navarro

How to Make Ethical and Moral Decisions: A Guide

Reiki The Instructors' Manual

Novels:

The Shaman's Quest

The Shaman's Transformation

The Shaman's Revelations

The Shaman's War

The Shaman's Genesis

The Making of a Shaman

DEDICATION

Teas, Soups & Salads Healing Recipes For
Supportive Medicine is dedicated to all those who
want to help heal themselves.

DISCLAIMER

This collection of recipes does not constitute medical advice in any way. You are responsible for how you use the information in this book. No information contained in this book should be considered "medical advice" and as with any recipe, you should check to make sure the ingredients do not have a negative impact on your well-being. If you have concerns, always check with your medical doctor. The intent here is supportive; not alternative.

Norman W. Wilson, Ph.D.

January 2020

INTRODUCTION

As a healer, I have long had an interest in recipes that help with one's healing processes. This short collection represents a select group of easy to create and easy to use recipes all of which are dedicated to being supportive of contemporary medical practices. This is not a diet book. It is a collection of recipes designed to give you a choice.

During the late 1900s, more was being said about alternative healing modalities leading to a full-blown alternative medicine industry. Among these alternative healing modalities are Yoga, Qu Gong, Acupuncture, Acupressure, Massage, Sound Massage, Meditation, Reiki, Shamanism, Ayurveda, Chiropractic, Body Movement Therapy, Tai chi, Electromagnetic Therapy, Hypnosis, Visualization and Guided Imagery, Emotional Freedom Technique (EFT or Tapping) Herbs, Essential Oils, and Diets. I note that recent literature now uses the acronym, CAM meaning complementary and alternative medicine. From my perspective, that's an improvement.

However, to be honest, I do not approve of the word *alternative* to describe other approaches to healing; some of which have been around for thousands of years. Because the word alternative suggests something other than and something that is better than current medical practice it denigrates the medical doctor and modern medical practices. I prefer complementary, integrated, or supportive medicine. At no time do I ever suggest or recommend that one by-pass medical treatment.

Medical drugs became chemically created rather than being plant-based. A drug is typically manufactured through chemical synthesis, which means that it is made by combining specific chemical ingredients in an ordered process. Because so many current drugs are chemically created and have myriad negative side effects many people seek other forms of treatment. The use of plant-based medicines in the United States has risen to 40% of all medicines produced. That is significant. It is estimated 80% of the populations of the developing nations use plant-based medicines. The prediction is 80% of the world's populations will rely upon plant-based medicines. It is in keeping with this trend that the following recipes for teas, soups, and salads are offered.

CHAPTER ONE-TEAS

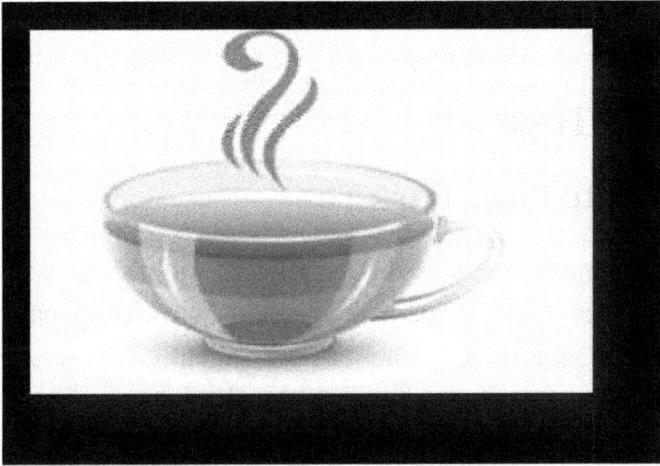

Tea is an aromatic beverage prepared by pouring hot water over dried plant leaves. The Chinese, during the Shang Dynasty, is credited with using tea as a medicinal drink. Third Century AD provides one of the earliest records of that use of tea. Hua Tuo wrote about tea's medicinal use in a medical text. However, it was not a popular drink until the Tang Dynasty. By the 1600 hundreds, tea was the fashionable drink among the English.

The following teas, all-natural, offer choice in flavor as well as in health benefits. As with all the recipes offered here, if you have allergies, high blood pressure, or any health issues that may conflict with the recipes offered, please be sure to consult your medical doctor before using any of them.

The Teas:

White Birch Bark Tea

The birch tree's bark, its leaves, and small twigs offer much in terms of healing. It helps lower pain, fever and is an excellent astringent. There are twelve species of this thin-leaved deciduous hardwood tree: Bog, Cherry, Downy, Dwarf, Himalayan, Japanese White, Paper (also called White Birch), River, Silver, Water, Weeping, and Yellow.

The bark and leaves, and small pieces of the branches may be eaten raw, cooked, or ground into a fine powder. Generally, the flavor is on the spicy side; wintergreen flavor, for example. The inner bark can be eaten and provides essential moisture to the human body. Because I am most familiar with the White Birch Tree or Paper Birch, it is the bark I use in making a healthy tea.

Directions:

Select four leaves, rinse thoroughly

Boil one cup of water

Crumple the four leaves into a cup

Pour the water over the leaves and let steep for about three minutes*

*If you prefer a strong tea, let it steep for five minutes. A nice addition, for those who prefer a sweeter tea, is a teaspoon of raw honey. By "raw" honey I mean one that has not been chemically processed.

Pine Tree Tea

Like the Birch Tree, there are many different species of Pine Trees, actually 115 different species throughout the world. The North American Continent is blessed with 36 Pine Tree species. Make sure you are not allergic to these stately and beautiful trees. And again, if you have questions or concerns always check with your medical doctor before drinking Pine Tree Tea. Because the needles of the Pine Tree are easily accessible I recommend using them as to the bark or pieces of branches. The needles are an excellent source of Vitamins C, E, A, and B. They are an excellent antimutagenic, that is, the Pine Needles prevent mutation and in this case, it is suggested cancer cells are prevented from mutating. The following URL provides further information (https://www.ncbi.nlm.nih.gov/pmc/articles/PMC5776635/).

Directions:

Rinse two to three cups of pine needles. Dry them.

Grind enough pine needles to make ½ cup

Boil 2 ½ cups of water

Place the ground pine needles in a teapot, add the boiling water, and let it steep for at least five minutes. For a stronger tea let it steep for eight to ten minutes.

To boost its flavor and healing capacity you may want to add a tablespoon of fresh lemon juice or lime juice and a tablespoon (or more) of raw honey.

As with all teas, sip, don't gulp.

Douglas Fir Tree Tea

The Douglas fir is an evergreen conifer species in the pine family and grows in size from a moderate height to extremely large evergreen *trees*, 70–330 feet tall. The Douglas has long, flat, spirally arranged needles that grow directly from the branch. As with the Pine, the Douglas Fir contains a good quantity of Vitamin C.

Its resin is an excellent antiseptic. The resin is obtained from the trunk of the tree. As a poultice, it is used to treat cuts, burns, wounds and other skin ailments. The young needle tips when used as flavoring in cooked foods offers up a woodsy flavor. The fresh leaves have a pleasant balsamic odor. The inner bark - dried, ground into a meal, may be added to cereals, and is good for making bread and biscuits.

A refreshing tea can be made from the young leaves.

<u>Directions:</u>

If you are selecting your own Douglas Fir, be sure to get the young fresh needles. Collect two full cups of the needles.

Thoroughly rinse the needles, making sure they are clean.

Dry the needles by placing them between two sheets of paper towels or spread them out on a cloth towel and pat them dry. Wait until they are completely dry. If you are in a hurry, spread the needles on a cookie sheet and place in an oven set at 175 degrees for 10 to 15 minutes. Check to make sure the needles aren't burning.

Grind the needles in a coffee grinder (one used for grinding herbs).

Depending on the number of cups and how strong you like your tea, place one to two tablespoons of the ground needles into a cup. Pour boiling water over the needles and let steep for five minutes.

The flavor will be earthy. If you want to tone the flavor down, add 1 teaspoon of fresh lemon or lime juice. For those who prefer a sweeter taste add one tablespoon of raw honey.

Stinging Nettle Tea

Since ancient times, Stinging Nettles have been used as medicine. Stinging is the operative word. Care must be taken in picking the leaves of the Nettles. Select the leaves closer to the top because they are the newer and fresher leaves. Use gloves to avoid being stung.

Nettles are loaded with excellent nutrients. Among these are Vitamins A, C, and K and several of the Bs. They contain calcium, iron, magnesium, and potassium as well as all of the Amino acids. Such a combination acts as antioxidants. In addition to acting as antioxidants, Stinging Nettles may help reduce inflammation, relieve hay fever, lower blood pressure, and may actually help control blood sugar.

There are potential negative side effects. First, be very careful when you pick the leaves. Their minuscule hairs sting and inject a variety of irritating chemicals: Acetylcholine, serotonin, and formic acids. Additionally, if you are taking blood thinners, blood pressure medicine, medicine for diabetes, or diuretics definitely talk with your medical doctor before consuming Stinging Nettles.

Directions:

If you pick your own Stinging Nettles, use gloves and wear long pants. Carefully, wash the leaves and dry them.

Combine dried seedless rosehip and dried mint leaves with the dried Stinging Nettle leaves. Place this in a teapot or cup, add boiling water and let steep for five minutes.

If you are making a single cup, use 1 teaspoon of the dry ingredients. If you are making a pot, use 1 tablespoon of the dry ingredients.

For additional taste add 1 teaspoon of lemon or lime juice and one tablespoon of raw honey.

Ginkgo Biloba Tea

Ginkgo biloba, commonly known as ginkgo or gingko, also known as the Maidenhair Tree, is the only living species in the division Ginkgophyta; all others of this species are extinct. We know that it has been around at least 270 million years because of the carbon dating of its remnants found in fossils. The tree is native to China where it is cultivated. It may help improve cognitive functions. Traditionally, its uses include soothing bladder infections and increased sexual energy. One study as reported in *JAMA* found that an extract of ginkgo Biloba, also known as EGb 761, was clinically effective in treating Alzheimer's dementia.

Directions:

In a teapot, add 1 tablespoon of Ginkgo Biloba, 1 tablespoon of Lemon Balm, 1 tablespoon of Holy Basil, and one slice of fresh lemon. To this add four cups of boiling water and let it steep for five to eight minutes.

Pour into a cup; add one thin slice of fresh ginger and one teaspoon of raw honey and stir.

People who use some types of antidepressants should not use Gingko Biloba. Again, check with your medical doctor.

Manchurian Mushroom Tea (Kombucha)

Manchurian Mushroom tea has the four main qualities that are necessary for numerous biological activities: detoxifying, protection against free-radical damage, energizing capabilities and the promotion of immunity. The drink is readily available at many stores.

Numerous benefits of drinking this cold tea have been espoused. There are now a good number of scientific studies being conducted to determine the benefits and potentially harmful aspects of this tea. Anecdotal records suggest the following benefits of Manchurian Mushroom Tea: Source of probiotics, contains antioxidants, kills bacteria, may reduce heart disease risk, may help manage Type 2 Diabetes, and may help protect against Cancer.

For those who choose to create their own you will need the following:

1 package of symbiotic bacteria and yeast culture (available at health food stores) and its starter liquid

2. One gallon of water

3. 2 Tablespoons of green tea

4. 1 tablespoon of cinnamon or vanilla or peppermint

5. 1 tablespoon of holy basil

6. 1 cup of sugar

7. A 1-gallon glass jug or jar

8. Cheesecloth

Directions:

Bring the water to a rolling boil. Add the tea, flavoring, and Holy Basil. Let this cool for at least one-half hour.

Add the tea and 1 cup of sugar to your glass jar.

Place the symbiotic bacteria and yeast culture on top of the tea mixture.

Add the starter liquid.

Cover the jar with cheesecloth and place it in a dark cabinet or cupboard.

Wait 2-3 weeks and then do a taste test.

You should note slight acidic sweet taste.

You may choose to let the tea sit a few days longer. This depends on your taste preference. If you are satisfied with the flavor and taste, pour the tea into smaller containers with lids. Refrigerate the Manchurian Tea.

Some make a habit of drinking a small glass of tea every day.

Holy Basil Tea

Holy Basil, commonly known as Tulasi or Tulsi, is native to the Indian subcontinent and is a widely spread cultivated plant throughout the Southeastern Asian tropics. Holy Basil is a green, leafy plant with purple flowers and is part of the mint family. It grows as an aromatic shrub. Holy Basil has a wide range of health benefits. Among the more predominate benefits are: reduction of anxiety, supportive of balanced blood sugar, heart health, improves sleep, improves skin health, improves brain functions, and promotes eye health.

Directions:

1 cup of water
¼ teaspoon of fennel seeds
¼ teaspoon of cumin
¼ teaspoon of cloves
¼ teaspoon of cardamom (crushed really fine)
½ teaspoon of Holy Basil
¼ teaspoon of rosebuds
¼ teaspoon of chamomile

Place all the ingredients in a small pot and let it simmer for 20 to 30 minutes.

Strain this into a mug. Add raw honey for sweetening. Add Almond Milk or Soy Milk if you like.

White Horehound and Crystal Tea

White horehound is a flowering plant in the mint family, native to Europe, northern Africa, and southwestern and central Asia, North and South America. A perennial, aromatic herb of the mint family, the plant has oval leaves covered with white, woolly hairs, and small, white flowers.

Traditionally, horehound has been used as a tonic for colds, in cough drops, liquors, and as a diuretic. Used with certain crystals it offers balance, general healing, and restoration.

Directions:

Choose a crystal that has relevance to you. Do not use selenite. It will dissolve in water. I prefer clear quartz or amethyst. Clear Quartz protects against negativity, helps one attune to one's higher self, and amplifies one's energy. Amethyst offers spiritual protection and purification and cleansing one's energy field of negative influences and attachments. It is acceptable to combine two or more crystals.

To make the crystal elixir, fill a medium-sized bowl, half full with fresh spring water.

Place your chosen crystals in a separate clean, clear glass.

Place the glass containing the crystals into the bowl of spring water.

Cover with cheesecloth. Set the bowl in sunlight or moonlight for 4 hours. If it is a cloudy day and no moon at night, let the covered bowl sit for at least 24 hours. Cool in the refrigerator overnight.

To make the crystal horehound tea, remove the cheesecloth cover from the bowl containing the jar with the crystal(s). Remove the jar containing the crystals. Pour the spring water in the pot and bring it to a full boil.

Pour a small amount of the boiling water into a teapot, swish it around, and then discard. Add 2 tablespoon of ground horehound leaves per cup to the teapot. I suggest you make enough for several cups. Add the rest of the boiling water. Let it steep for at least 5 minutes; longer if you prefer stronger tea.

Strain the crystal horehound tea through a mesh strainer or use a piece of cheesecloth.

You may add honey, a sprig of fresh peppermint, or ginger, or a slice of fresh lemon to your tea. Pour the remaining tea into a jar, seal it, and refrigerate. Next time you want a cup of crystal horehound tea you have some already made and waiting to be drunk.

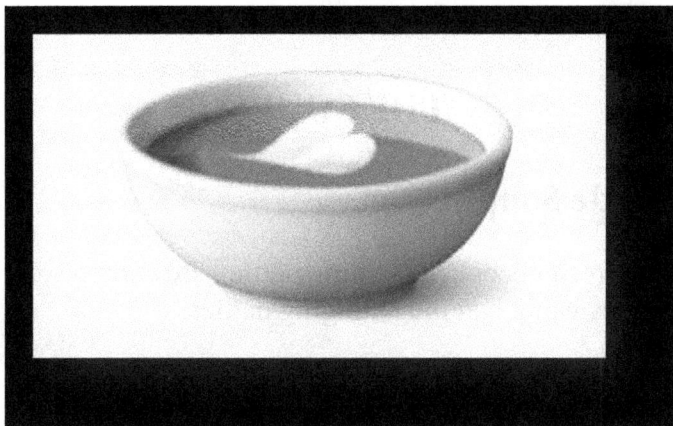

CHAPTER TWO-SOUPS

Soups have been around probably since the beginning of humankind. Whatever their history, soups evolved depending upon what local ingredients were readily available, and of course, dependent on local, regional, and personal tastes. We have Spanish Gazpacho, Russian Borscht, and Minestrone from Italy, Chinese Won-Ton, and New England Chowder. The soups offered here are all based on what they can do to help keep you healthy.

THE SOUPS

Nettle Soup

Use fresh uncooked stinging nettles. Be sure to wear gloves while handling stinging nettles.

Ingredients:

Fill a 5-gallon bucket with the stinging nettles
1 teaspoon of coarse salt
1 tablespoon of extra virgin olive oil or Avocado Oil
1 tablespoon of butter
½ cup of chopped onions
½ cup of chopped celery
4 good sized white potatoes, peeled and chopped
5 cups of chicken stock
2 to 3 cups of water
1 bay leaf
A couple of sprigs of fresh thyme
2 cloves of fresh garlic, peeled and chopped
Pepper (Your choice as to the amount)
The juice of one lemon

<u>Directions:</u>

Fill a large pot with water, add a teaspoon of salt, and bring the water to a rapid boil. Fill a large bowl with ice water. Be sure you are wearing gloves; transfer the Nettles to the boiling water. Cook for about 2 minutes. Use tongs to remove the nettles and place them in the ice water.

Strain the nettles into a colander.

Generally, by blanching the nettles they should have lost their sting; however, I would still use the gloves to sort the nettles for any large stems. Cut those and discard them.

Collect 4 or 5 cups of the blanched nettles. Set this aside.

Use a 6-quart pot; add the olive oil and butter. Heat on medium. Add the chopped onions and celery. Cook until softened, about 5 or 6 minutes.

Add the potatoes, chicken stock, and spices. Simmer for 5 or 6 minutes.

Chop the nettles and add these to the pot and add enough water to cover the nettles and potatoes. Return to simmer and simmer for 15 to 20 minutes.

Check to make sure the potatoes are soft and the nettles are tender.

Remove the bay leaf and purée the soup. Return this to the pot, turn off the heat. Stir in the lemon juice and serve. You may want to swirl in some cream just as you serve the soup and add some fresh parsley.

Watercress Soup

As a part of the vegetable group that includes kale, Brussels sprouts, and cabbage, watercress is often overlooked despite the fact that it is loaded with powerful nutrients. Among these nutrients are Vitamins A, C, and K. Calcium and Manganese are also included. One cup of watercress contains over 100% of the RDI for Vitamin K. Additionally; watercress is loaded with antioxidants that protect against cell damage.

In terms of taste, the flavor of watercress is slightly peppery and spicy.

Ingredients:

2 to 3 tablespoons of butter
2 cups of yellow onion, coarsely chopped
Salt (to taste)
1 cup of white wine, or vegetable stock for those who are vegetarian, chicken stock for those who are not
3 to 4 white potatoes, peeled and cut into chunks
6 cups of water
6 cups of watercress, chopped (stems included)
Pepper (to taste)
4 tablespoons of sour cream

Directions:

In a large pot, melt the butter, add the onions and cook over medium heat until they are soft. Cook for about 5 to 6 minutes. Add salt to the onions. (I don't add salt to my cooking. Adding salt is your choice.)

Add the potatoes and whichever liquid you have chosen (white wine, vegetable broth or chicken broth) and bring to a quick boil.

Turn the heat down to low, cover the pop, and let simmer for about 30 minutes. Check to see if the potatoes are done.

Add the watercress, stir well, and cook for another 2 to 3 minutes.

Remove from the heat and purée. CAUTION: Be careful with hot liquids.

Season to taste and add the sour cream. If you want to go a bit fancy, don't stir in the sour cream in the pot; add a tablespoon to each cup as you serve it.

Coconut Carrot Ginger Soup

Ginger is a flowering plant whose root is widely used as a spice and in supportive medicine. It is part of the same plant family as cardamom, galangal, and turmeric and is produced in India, Fiji, Australia, and Indonesia. Ginger is an anti-inflammatory and antioxidant food and is considered to be one of the world's healthiest foods. It is suggested that ginger helps fight certain types of cancer, Alzheimer's, and heart diseases. Because ginger is a mild stimulate it is recommended that you do not consume large quantities before retiring. If you are on medications, check with your doctor before consuming ginger because it has a tendency to increase the action of some medications.

Ingredients:

1 tablespoon of extra virgin olive oil
1 tablespoon of butter
1 medium yellow onion, diced
2 ½ c garlic cloves, minced
2 ½ pounds of trimmed, peeled, and chopped carrots
1 two-inch piece of fresh ginger, grated
6 cups of water or chicken broth (vegetable broth may be used in place of the chicken broth)
1 ¼ cups of coconut milk
½ cup of croutons for topping if desired

Directions:

Heat the olive oil and butter in a large pot. Add the onions and garlic. Cook about 4 minutes over medium heat. The onions should be translucent. Stir frequently to ensure even cooking. Add the carrots.

Add the water, or chicken or vegetable broth. Cook, covered, over medium-high heat for about 30-40 minutes, depending on the size of the carrots.

Remove the pot from the heat, let its contents cool, and then add the coconut milk. Bled the ingredients until smooth and nice and creamy.

Serve in warmed bowls or cups. Add a sprinkle of the croutons.

Rutabaga Soup

The root vegetable, rutabaga is known by several names: Turnip, neep, and swede. In reality, the rutabaga is a cross between a cabbage and a turnip. The rutabaga is loaded with Vitamin C, E, as well as Potassium and Magnesium. It is high in fiber. They are an excellent source of antioxidants.

Ingredients:

4 fully packed tablespoons of butter
1 medium-sized yellow onion, coarsely chopped
3 stalks of celery, coarsely chopped. (Wash the celery before using.)
2 to 3 good sized rutabagas, peeled and coarsely chopped
4 to 6 cups of vegetable broth or if you prefer, chicken broth, or bone broth
2 to 3 teaspoons of smoked paprika

Directions:

Melt the butter in a good-sized pot. Let the butter foam up and when it does add the chopped onion and celery. Continue to cook, occasionally stirring until the vegetables are tender. Don't let them brown. This should take about 5 or 6 minutes.

Add the rutabagas and broth of your choice. Bring to a boil, and then reduce the heat to low to simmer. Continue cooking until the rutabagas are tender. Check them by piercing with a fork. Cook for about 30 or 35 minutes.

Add the half and half, paprika and stir until thoroughly mixed.

Remove from heat, let cool a bit, and then purée.

It may be necessary to purée more than one batch.

Salt and pepper to taste.

Beet Soup

Beets are an excellent source of fiber, Vitamin B9, manganese, potassium, iron and Vitamin C. Beets and their juice have long been associated with health benefits, many of which are due to the beets high concentrate of inorganic nitrates. Among the many health benefits are improved blood flow and lower blood pressure.

Ingredients:

4 to 6 medium-sized beets, leaves, and stems removed and the roots on the bottom removed. Cut in half.
3 to 4 cups of water
3 cups of coarsely chopped cabbage
2 medium-sized white potatoes, peeled and diced
1 large carrot, peeled and thinly sliced rounds
2 stalks of cleaned celery, thinly sliced
1 good sized yellow onion chopped
1 teaspoon minced garlic
1 bay leaf,
1 cup of sour cream. Be sure it has been at room temperature for an hour before using
Several sprigs of fresh dill
Salt and Pepper

Directions:

In a large pot, add the water and beets. Bring to a boil, reduce to a simmer. Cook until beets are tender. Use a fork to check its doneness. Remove the beets and set them aside.

To the remaining liquid add the cabbage, potatoes, onion, celery, and garlic and bay leaf. Bring back to a boil, reduce the heat and simmer, uncovered, for at least 35 minutes. Check the vegetables to make sure they are tender.

When the vegetables are done, remove and discard the bay leaf.

Purée the soup. You may have to do more than one batch.

Pour into a large pan, whisk in the sour cream, making sure it is well blended. Gently, reheat the soup.

Serve in warm bowls or cups and garnish with the dill.

Maitake Mushroom Soup

First and foremost, the Maitake is an adaptogen; that is, it helps one's body in fighting mental and physical difficulties. Maitake grows wild in Japan, China and the continent of North America. It grows at the bottom of Oak, Elm, and Maple trees. If you are adept at identifying wild plants, look for this mushroom in the fall months.

The Maitake is rich in antioxidants, beta-glucans, Vitamins B and C, copper, potassium, amino acids, fiber, and minerals. Research since 2013 has suggested the Maitake Mushroom helps with cholesterol issues, type 2 diabetes, and in fighting breast cancer.

Ingredients:

6 to 8 ounces of Maitake Mushrooms, chopped
½ pound of fresh common mushrooms
3 to 4 tablespoons of extra virgin olive oil
3 shallots, chopped
1 leek, chopped
1 medium yellow onion, chopped
2 stalks of cleaned celery, chopped
1 to 2 carrots, chopped (If the carrot is large use one)
1 medium-sized white potato, peeled and chopped
4 to 6 cups of vegetable, or chicken stock, or water
2 to 3 tablespoons of tamari sauce (add more or less depending on personal taste)

1 bay leaf
2 teaspoons of chopped fresh thyme
1 teaspoon of chopped fresh rosemary
Salt and Pepper to taste

Directions:

Heat the oil in a large pot, medium heat

Add the Maitake Mushrooms, shallot, leek, onion, celery, carrot, potato, and common mushrooms. Increase the heat to a medium-high and cook for ten minutes or until the vegetables begin to soften

Add the stock (vegetable, chicken, or water), tamari, bay leaf and bring to a boil. Reduce heat and let simmer for 30 to 35 minutes.

Add the thyme and rosemary.

Purée. Use caution when pureeing hot foods.

Season to taste with salt and pepper.

Serve in heated soup bowls or cups. For garnish, add a sprig of fresh mint, or parsley.

Cauliflower Vegetable Soup

There are several health aids one may derive from eating cauliflower. Because it contains Vitamin C which helps with collagen production and it's Vitamin K makes cauliflower an excellent vegetable to help prevent bone loss. Additionally, cauliflower contains Indole-3-carbinol, a phytonutrient. This has been shown to be helpful to the liver in its detox functions. Consumption of cauliflower can help boost one's HDL (that's the good kind) and lower blood pressure. Interestingly enough, it contains Choline which helps maintain gastrointestinal health and glutathione, an antioxidant that helps fight off infections. And finally, because cauliflower's Indole-3-carbinols and sulforaphane help protect cells from DNA damage, it may help reduce the risk of cancer.

Ingredients:

1 large head of cauliflower
3 tablespoons of extra virgin olive oil
1 medium sweet onion, chopped
1 leek (chop only the white and pale green parts)
3 carrots, chopped
1 large white potato, peeled and chopped
2 stalks of celery, chopped
6 to 8 cups of vegetable or chicken stock
1 bay leaf
1 branch of fresh thyme
¼ cup of cilantro or dill or basil, chopped

Directions:

Cut the head of cauliflower into florets; set these aside. You should have several cups full.

Chop the remaining cauliflower into about one-inch chunks

Heat the extra virgin olive oil in a large pot; medium heat
Add the onion, leeks, carrots, potato, celery, and the one-inch cauliflower chunks. Cook for 6 to 8 minutes or until the onion is translucent

Add the broth, bay leaf, thyme

Bring the soup to a boil, cover and reduce to a simmer. Cook for about 20 minutes. It could take a bit longer, depending on the vegetables.

Remove from the heat; discard the bay leave and the twig of thyme.

Blend the soup Be careful in handling the hot soup mixture.

Remove the soup from the blender, add the cauliflower florets, and cook an additional 10 minutes.

Carefully pour the soup into heated bowls or cups, sprinkle on the cilantro, or dill, or basil. Salt and Pepper to taste.

Four and a half cup Chilled Tomato Soup

This deliciously chilled soup contains three spices that offer wonderful healing minerals: Potassium, calcium, magnesium, iron, and Vitamin C, B6, and folate.

Cardamom, native to Southern India, is considered to be one of the oldest spices in the world. It's use dates back to 4000 years ago.

Cumin, used by the Ancient Egyptians in their mummification processes, offers antioxidants.

Cayenne Pepper, from French Guiana, is now largely produced in India and Mexico, has long been associated with pain reduction.

Ingredients:

1 28-ounce can of whole peeled tomatoes with liquid (Because many canned tomatoes contain a lot of sodium, I suggest a non-sodium or at least a low sodium brand such as Cento San Marzano Whole Peeled Tomatoes.)
2 tablespoons of extra virgin olive oil
½ teaspoon of each of these spices: cardamom, cumin, cayenne (More may be added to accommodate individual taste)
1 yellow onion chopped
3 cloves of garlic minced

1 ½ cups of nonfat plain yogurt
1 teaspoon of lemon juice (lime juice if you prefer)

Directions:

In a nonstick skillet, heat the olive oil over medium-high heat. Add cardamom, cumin, and cayenne pepper. Stir until the smells become noticeably fragrant. No more than 30 seconds. 35 seconds maximum.

Add the chopped onion and minced garlic. Reduce the heat to medium and cook until the onion softens; about 5 or 6 minutes. Don't let it burn or brown up.

Add the full 28-ounce can of low-sodium tomatoes with the juice. Bring to a simmer and cook for 10 or 12 minutes.

Remove from heat, and let cool for about 5 minutes.

Stir in the yogurt and lemon juice. Be sure to work in the yogurt into the mixture.

Purée mixture, pour into a large bowl. Repeat the process until all the soup has been puréed.

Cover the bowl, refrigerate until well chilled. Probably a good 30 minutes, depending on your refrigerator's settings.

Serve chilled in a bowl or cup. Add a sprig of fresh rosemary for garnish.

Salt and Pepper to taste.

CHAPTER THREE-SALADS

It is reported that the word salad is derived from the Latin *sal*, the word for salt. The basis for this the use of leafy vegetables dressed with salt and an oily dressing. The food concept of salad is credited to the Roman Empire.

For those of you who would like a more in-depth discussion of the origins of salad here are two sources:
https://www.huffpost.com/entry/evolution-of-the-salad_n_7101632 and

https://www.encyclopedia.com/sports-and-everyday-life/food-and-drink/food-and-cooking/salads.

The Salads:

Fresh Spinach Salad:

Spinach originated in Persia and belongs to the same family relation as beets and quinoa. Spinach is loaded with nutrients and antioxidants. Additionally, Spinach is an excellent source of Vitamins A, C, K1, and B9. Iron, calcium, lutein, kaempferol, nitrates, quercetin, and zeaxanthin are also present in Spinach.

There are many recipes for spinach salad. The following recipe is simple to make and takes very little time.

Ingredients:

4 cups of Spinach. This recipe is for two people.
Dressing:
3 tablespoons of extra virgin olive oil
1 tablespoon of regular vinegar
½ teaspoon of garlic powder
½ teaspoon of oregano
½ teaspoon of celery salt

Directions:

Even though the bag containing the spinach says it has been cleaned and ready to use, I always wash the spinach in water and then spin it dry. If you don't have a spinner, use a clean towel to pat the spinach dry.

In a small dish or a bottle, thoroughly mix the ingredients for the dressing.

Spoon the dressing over the spinach and serve.

To up the nutritional values add almonds.

Carrot Salad with a Twist

Fresh carrots, often said to be perfect health food, is an excellent source of beta carotene, fiber, Vitamin K1, potassium, and antioxidants. Carrots provide Vitamin A, Biotin (formerly called Vitamin H), potassium, and Vitamin B6. Eating carrots provides a number of health benefits. Among these are weight-loss, linked to a reduced risk of cancer, lower cholesterol, and improved eye health.

Ingredients:

4 medium-sized carrots, peeled
1 fennel bulb
¼ cup slivered toasted almonds
¼ cup of fresh lemon juice (lime if you prefer)
2 tablespoons of raw honey

Directions:

Using a food processor coarsely grate carrots. You can chop them if you prefer our use a grater. Place these in a bowl.

Slice the fennel bulb into thin slices and chops the fronds. **Fronds** are frilly green leafy things attached to the stalks that grow out of a fennel bulb. Add these to the carrots.

Add the fresh lemon juice, raw honey, and toasted almonds.

Gently mix and serve.

Chopped Radish

Used for Centuries in folk medicine, in Ayurveda, and Chinese medicine, radishes were used to treat sore throat, fevers, and inflammation. In today's world, we know they are a good source of Vitamin C and do seem to have other health qualities. A study, done in 2010, found that radishes contained isothiocyanates that kill some cancer cells. Further, radishes support a healthy digestive system and are antifungal.

Besides the red round radishes, radishes also come in white, purple, or black.

Ingredients:

2 bunches of radishes with stems and leaves
4 to 6 ounces of feta cheese or blue cheese if you want a richer taste
1 yellow onion or red onion if you prefer
12 green olives (ripe if you prefer)
2 tablespoons of extra virgin olive oil
1 to 2 ounces of dry white wine (for a non-alcoholic recipe, used vinegar)

Directions:

Clean the radishes, cutting away the stems and leaves

Cut each radish into at least 4 pieces, place in a bowl

Chop the onion, add to the radishes

Cut the olives in half and add to the bowl

Add the olive oil and white wine

Add the cheese, and gently mix all the ingredients.

Serve. (For an enhancement consider placing on a bed of lettuce and offer Oregano crackers. Add a favorite beverage, perhaps a quality red wine.

Kale Salad with Walnuts

Kale, originating in the eastern Mediterranean, has been around at least since 2,000 BC. It ranks among the most nutrient of foods, and as such, it is said to have all sorts of beneficial compounds. There are several types of Kale; some with green leaves while others have purple leaves and some have curly leaves while others are smooth. The most common type of Kale is Curly Kale or as it is sometimes called Scots Kale.

Kale is loaded with the following Vitamins: A, K, C, B6, and Manganese, Calcium, Copper, Potassium, and Magnesium. It has powerful antioxidants Quercetin and Kaempferol. Its Lutein and Zeaxanthin hare excellent eye nutrients

The benefits of eating Kale include cholesterol and cancer-fighting substances.

Ingredients:

2 washed bunches of kale with stems removed and cut into small pieces. (You may need to add more of everything if you are serving more than two people).
¼ cup of extra virgin olive oil
¼ cup of chopped onion (yellow, white, or red)

½ cup of coarsely chopped walnuts. (or pecans, almonds, cashews)
½ teaspoon of lemon or lime juice
Salt and Pepper to taste.

To add a bit more flavoring you may want to roast the walnuts.

Directions:

Tear the Kale into small pieces and place in a bowl. Add the stems.

Add the olive oil and lemon juice

Add the chopped onion

Add the walnuts

Mix well

Serve on a plate or in a bowl. If you use a plate, to add to the display, add two slices of the lemon along the edge.

Arugula-Radicchio Salad

Arugula is native to the Mediterranean region. It has been a popular cuisine ingredient in Italy, Morocco, Portugal, and Turkey, and there is evidence it was used in Ancient Egypt and Rome. Brought to America by British colonists but it was not until the late 1990's that it became popular in the United States. In India, its seeds are used to make Taramira that is used for medicinal purposes.

Radicchio has been around for a very long time, also. Pliny the Elder is credited to be the first to write about it. (23 A.D. to 79A. D. There are 5 different types of radicchio. Radicchio di Chioggia is the one most easily found in local grocery stores.

Endive supposedly originated in Egypt or Indonesia back during the 16th century. However, the official version of the story, however, is different. It seems that in 1830 it was discovered in Belgium by a farmer named Jan Lammers. Thus, we have Belgian endive. It is also rich in vitamins and minerals, especially folate, vitamins A and K, and is also high in fiber.

The consumption of these three vegetables is said to reduce the risk of diabetes, heart disease, and the presence of Vitamin K helps with blood clotting and helps prevent the risk of osteoporosis. It is said that it helps lower the risk of lung and colon cancers. The Sulforaphane contained in these vegetables has a promise in impeding melanoma, esophageal, prostate, and pancreatic cancers. For those who are taking blood-thinners such as warfarin, be careful not to overeat vegetables containing Vitamin K.

Ingredients:

1 to 2 packages of arugula, thoroughly wash and drain
1 radicchio, remove the core and cut into ½ inch slices
2 to 3 garlic cloves, minced (depending on taste, less or more may be used)
3 to 4 tablespoons of extra virgin olive oil (at room temperature)
2 tablespoons of balsamic vinegar
2 to 3 ounces of Parmesan cheese, grated or shaved
1 head endive, cut into ½ inch slices (before slicing, thoroughly rinse the endive and pat dry)

Directions:

In a large bowl add the olive oil, balsamic vinegar, garlic, and mix thoroughly. Add the arugula, radicchio, endive. Toss, making sure all leaves are covered.

Divide, and serve on plates. Grate the Parmesan cheese over each.

You may wish to add three or four turmeric crackers to each plate.

Red Tomato Salad

Tomatoes have origin traced back to the early Aztecs around 700 A.D. It appears the tomato was introduced to Europe in the 1500 BC by explorers returned from traveling to new lands. As a consequence, the tomato is considered to be native to the Americas. Despite the fact that for a couple of centuries the tomato was considered poisonous, it is now the 4th most popular vegetable in the United States.

Tomatoes have a high nutritional value. They help lower the risk of developing heart diseases, diabetes, and cancer. It has essential potassium that is crucial to blood pressure. Tomatoes are helpful to good eye health, and skin.

There are risks. Tomatoes are rich in potassium. That may cause an issue with certain types of medications prescribed for heart issues. Too much potassium can be harmful to people with kidney issues.

Ingredients:

4 to 5 medium ripe red tomatoes, washed
½ red onion, sliced into thin circles
1dozen fresh basil leaves washed
1 to 2 tablespoons of extra virgin olive oil

2 cloves of garlic, minced
12 green olives, cut in half (black olives, if you prefer)
2 mushrooms, sliced
6 crackers (your choice as to kind) or two rolls, warmed.

Directions:

Cut the washed tomatoes into 1-inch cubes, place in a large bowl.

Add the sliced red onion, olive oil, garlic, olives, and mushrooms (you may eliminate the mushrooms)

Carefully, turn the ingredients around in the bowl.

Place on plates or in bowls, serve with the crackers or rolls.

Two Beans Salad

According to the Seed Savers Exchange, based in Iowa, there are over 4,000 varieties of beans. So, which of these beans have been selected for this salad? Both green and yellow beans have been selected as the beans of choice.

Green beans originated in Peru and from there spread throughout the Americas. Spanish explorers introduced this bean to Europe in the 16th Century according to the University of Arizona. The Green Bean has been cultivated in Mexico for at least 7,000 years.

Its history, flavor, and as a source for Vitamins A, C, K, and folic acid, and fiber makes this bean a natural choice for a salad.

The yellow bean (yellow wax) was from the area of Algeria. This bean, like the green bean, is rich in fiber, Vitamin A and C, B1, B3, E, K, manganese, magnesium, and potassium.

There are potential risks in eating this salad for those who are taking blood-thinners because of the amount of Vitamin K. If you have a mineral deficiency be sure an check with your medical doctor before consuming green and or yellow wax beans.

Ingredients:

2 cups fresh green beans, washed and cut into thirds (trimmed)
2 cups of fresh yellow wax beans, washed, and cut into thirds (trimmed)
2 tablespoons of extra virgin olive oil
6 ounces of mozzarella cheese, sliced (Be sure it is made from water buffalo milk)
½ cup of washed basil leaves, chopped medium
4 tablespoons of pine nuts

Directions:

In a large pot, add six quarts of water, a dash of salt, bring to a boil and add the beans. Cook about for three or four minutes.

Drain, immediately fill the pot with cold tap water and add several ice cubes. You want to stop the cooking as quickly as possible to ensure a crisp bean. Using a colander, drain the beans, and then separate the two beans; place them on a towel to dry.

Spread the pine nuts on a baking sheet. Heat your oven to 275 degrees. Roast the pine nuts for about 7 minutes. You should smell their fragrance and they should look a golden color.

Transfer the beans to a medium-sized bowl, add the olive oil, and toss.

Slice the mozzarella into 4 to 6 thin round slices. Cut each of these in half.

Using 4 salad plates divide the cheese slices and beans on the plates, alternate the green and yellow beans with the cheese.

Sprinkle a generous amount of the basil and pine nuts on each salad and serve with a warm roll or your favorite crackers. Add a glass of your favorite red wine.

Greek Salad

The basis of this delicious salad is cucumber. Originating in India the cucumber has been a cultivated vegetable for 3,000 years or more.

Because cucumbers are 95% water, they are an excellent way to keep you hydrated. Additionally, they contain potassium, Vitamins C, A, and K. They are a natural source of magnesium and manganese. They also contain two phytonutrient compounds associated with anti-cancer benefits: lignans and cucurbitacins.

Current concerns over pesticides and wax on cucumbers create the suggestion that one should only use organically grown cucumbers.

Ingredients:

2 to 3 cups of fresh green beans, trimmed
1 head of Romaine Lettuce, coarsely chopped
1 to 2 medium-sized cucumbers, thoroughly washed, cut lengthwise. Remove the seeds and thinly sliced into 4 strips
1 medium-sized red onion, peeled and thinly sliced
4 to 6 ounces of crumbled Feta Cheese
2 to 3 ripe but firm tomatoes, washed thoroughly, cut into wedges

½ cup of pitted Kalamata Olives, sliced in half (Any olive will work if you don't have Kalamata readily available)
½ cup chopped parsley,
Salt & Pepper to taste

The Dressing:

2 cloves of garlic, finely minced
1 teaspoon of oregano
2 tablespoons of Agiorgitiko, a Greek Red Wine
2 tablespoons of red wine vinegar
4 to 6 tablespoons of extra virgin olive oil
1 teaspoon of celery salt
Mix all ingredients thoroughly

The Directions:

Place all the salad ingredients into a large bowl, mix well

Put equal amounts on plates, drizzle the dressing over each salad

Serve with warmed Greek bread and a glass of Agiorgitiko.

7 Cups of Tea

The first cup moistens the throat;

The second cup shatters all feelings of solitude;

The third cup cleans the digestion, and brings to mind the wisdom of 5,000 volumes;

The four induces perspiration, evaporating all of life's trials and tribulations; with the fifth cut, body sharpens, crisp;

And the sixth cup is the first on the road to enlightenment;

The seventh cup sits steaming—it needn't be drunk, as from head to feet one rises to the abode of the immortals.

Lu Tong, 9th Century

ABOUT THE AUTHOR

Norman Wilson, a retired college professor, is a shaman and a Reiki Master, is a certified crystal healer, and is trained in the use of herbs and essential oils.